To Myra.

love,

DEDICATED TO THE
MEMORY OF
SICA ELLSMORE
ATRICK O'BRIEN
REE SPO)

EATING THE INDIES

A WRESTLING COOKBOOK

WRITTEN BY HAYLEY MILLER
COVER BY CATHERINE PEREZ
DESIGNED BY DAVID MACHADO
RECIPE CONSULTATION BY CAMILLA LEWIS
EDITED BY STEVEN BRADLEY

DEDICATED TO THE
MEMORY OF
JESSICA ELLSMORE
& SEAN PATRICK O'BRIEN
(REFEREE SPO)

2.5.1987 - 3.2.2023   10.6.1988 - 3.17.2023

Independent wrestling was named for the fact that it existed 'independently' of WWE or big TV money. It has always been a tradition that is kept alive because of the love of the industry, the talent and the incredible stories that are told year in and year out. However, I would argue that the word independent is no longer accurate in describing what we all love so much. In actual fact it is the unity of people that keeps the industry alive and thriving. A collective spirit of different people coming together to create art, whether it be wrestlers, writers, photographers or even the fans, everyone has a role to play.

It is the people who dedicate their lives around the industry that I have the utmost respect for. Spending hundreds of hours on the road, being away from family and sacrificing what many would describe as a normal life all for the love of professional wrestling. It is those people that inspired the creation of this book.

I wanted to connect you to the people behind the gimmicks and the best way to truly connect to a person is through the food that they eat. Food can tell us so much about a person, their culture and what brings them happiness and now you have the opportunity to try these recipes for yourself.

Eating The Indies is a celebration of the Indies. Wrestlers, writers, designers and everything in between.

Personally, I want to thank everyone that supported this project. Whether you backed the Kickstarter or just dropped a nice word about it on Twitter, I appreciate you.

This project was 10% me and 90% David Machado and Haley Miller. It simply would not exist without them. David is an incredibly talented designer and Haley is a wonderful writer. They both have big futures and I'm so honored to have them involved.

Finally, a huge thank you to my son Preston and my wife Diana for their constant support of my various obsessions. I appreciate you putting up with me.

All the best, enjoy the food.

Steven
(@OaklandRovers)

Eating The Indies would not have been possible without the following people that could only be described as Main Event Level supporters of independent Wrestling.

Felicia Gordon	Jack Rabin	Rebecca Freidel
Richard Downing	Don Becker	Sam Deetz
Michael Cervino	Jim Quartuccio	Blake McMillan (50 Foot Blake)
Joe Fitzpatrick	Iam Thompson	The Buckley's
Tamaya Greenlee	Dan Pascsale	Mike
Paddy Jones	Rob Kamerer	Craig Danks
Steve Pillmeier	Travis Hurt	Matt Sheppard
Jamielynn Ciccone	Ana Bird	Joseph Cardamon ||
Ido Sela	Stacy Fowler	Kelson
Russ Burlingame	Shane Simon	Heather and Michael Royston
Sam Teller	Mark Leslie	Aaron Carlisle
Wayne P Witkowski	Shawn McMahon	Kim Hamilton
Chris Creamer	Robert Williams	Farmer Jake Richard
Kiersten Cline	Rory Starks	Kevin McElvaney (PWI)
Wendy Bradley	Max Gadson	Margaret McCarthy
Charles Cook	Ally Nicole	Shawn Freeman
Brian Ginzberg	Lucy Gliddon	Wayne Freeman
Roberto Chacon	Sloane Webber	Wesley Johnson
Joey Goller	Justin Ruff	Roy Bangs
Katie Surridge	Heath Freidel	Alex Castillo (Vinyls & Violence)

Thank You.

MAIN EVENT SPONSORS

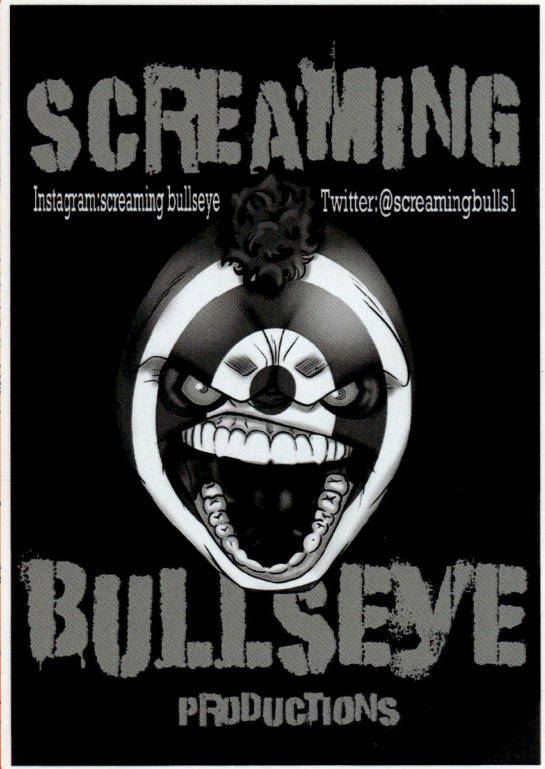

SCREAMING BULLSEYE PRODUCTIONS

LAROCK CREATIONS

SIMON BABYCAT SOAP CO.
SIMONBABYCATSOAPCO.BIGCARTEL.COM

OFFICIAL PODCAST

YOUR DOSE OF DEATH
PODCAST

TERRA CALAWAY

Terra Calaway was born in Las Vegas, Nevada, and she now resides on the East Coast. Inside the ring, Calaway has been a powerhouse in the professional wrestling industry for over a decade that breaks down barriers for women's wrestlers all over the world. Calaway has held various titles over her career and as of writing, is the current and second longest reigning ISDub Undisputed King Of Crazy Champion. Calaway placed #59 in the QWI 200 in 2021 and #67 in 2022.

Outside, Calaway holds many hats. As an activist, advocate, founder of Dropkick Depression (a charity non-profit promotion), and author of the Women of the Deathmatch zine and her various Mental Health zines, there's nothing she can't do! Calaway and her husband live in a meat-free household. In our interview, she discusses what the initial transition was like and how it changed her perspective on food.

When did you make the switch to vegetarianism and was it as smooth of a transition as you had hoped?

Ever since I started dating my husband, I leaned more toward vegetarianism because he's vegan. So it wasn't a cold turkey one day tossing it all out. I was phasing it out for years. I really only ate chicken for the most part. Then at the start of 2022, I decided there was no real reason I was still eating meat so I completely changed over. It was definitely smooth because of the years of weaning myself off of it.

Is it a dish you whip out at a gathering to impress the guests?

Very much so. My husband is vegan as are a lot of his friends, so being able to adapt the recipe no matter who is eating it is definitely my favorite little trick up my sleeve.

When do you crave it the most?

Whenever we're going to some form of potluck or party. If I don't have time to make it or if we're told not to bring anything, I always feel like I'm missing it. Honestly, after writing up the recipe and getting it ready for this book, it's making me want it!

How has the vegan/vegetarian lifestyle changed your perspective on cooking and food in general?

I think I really appreciate the art of cooking food so well that you can feed it to someone who likes to shun the plant-based lifestyle and they'd never have a clue. Half of the food at our wedding was vegan, including the cake, and not a single person who eats meat could tell. It's really an art to be able to cook like that and I appreciate it. I can't cook like that, but I can certainly enjoy it!

Is there a piece of chef-y wisdom you've learned that you'd like to impart to the readers?

Slower is better. I tried to cook this quickly and would end up with weird little chunks of unmelted cheese. Also, cooking it on high heat has a higher probability of you burning the cheese. Take your time! Also, with the whole slow thing, if you have extra of this dip - Eat it the next day. The extra time in the cheese makes the spices just THAT much better. 10/10.

TERRA CALAWAY'S
VEG BEEFY QUESO
INGREDIENTS NEEDED:

SERVES: 4-6 | PREP TIME: 5 MINS | COOK TIME: 10 MINS.

- MILK (REGULAR OR PLANT BASED)
- 16 OZ. BLOCK OF VELVEETA CHEESE
- 1 BAG OF VEG BEEF CRUMBLES (GARDEIN PREFERRED)
- PAPRIKA
- CAYENNE PEPPER
- CHILI POWDER
- CUMIN
- LIME JUICE
- JALAPENO JUICE

INSTRUCTIONS

1. CUBE CHEESE

2. ADD CUBED CHEESE TO A SAUCE PAN WITH 1 CUP OF MILK ON MEDIUM HEAT. (MAKE SURE TO STIR AS YOU ADD INGREDIENTS)

3. ADD 2 TSP OF PAPRIKA, 1/2 TSP OF GROUND CAYENNE PEPPER, 4 TSP OF CHILI POWDER, AND 1/2 TSP OF GROUND CUMIN.

4. ONCE MIXED ADD VEG BEEF CRUMBLES.

5. STIR UNTIL CHEESE IS COMPLETELY MELTED (IF YOU WANT THE CHEESE THINNER ADD MILK TO YOUR PREFERRED CONSISTENCY)

6. ADD 1 TSP OF LIME JUICE AND 1 TSP OF JALAPENO JUICE.

7. STIR UNTIL COMPLETELY MIXED AND TRANSFER INTO A BOWL.

8.

PHOTO BY PILEDRIVER PHOTO

KASEY KIRK

Kasey Catal, also known as Kasey Kirk, is making waves on the Deathmatch wrestling scene. Synonymous with Mariah Carey's "Fantasy" and a staple for companies like ICW, in September of 2022, Catal became the ICW American Deathmatch Champion at ICW No Holds Barred Volume 32. There, she defeated renowned Deathmatch wrestler Joel Bateman in a career-defining match and would hold the title for nearly 100 days. Catal has only been wrestling professionally since 2017 and outside of Deathmatch wrestling, Catal is one-half of the longest-reigning (as of this writing) WSU Tag Team Champions with Delmi Exo. She has also held titles in Empower Wrestling and Synergy Pro Wrestling.

First making a name for herself in CZW, gaining a following as part of "The Office" stable. Catal has also won various tournaments, including the Cannabis Cup, the IWA Dutch Double Death Tag Team Tournament, and Pro Wrestling After Dark's Violence For The Sake Of. Catal trained at Create A Pro Academy under the guidance of Brian Myers and Pat Buck. In 2023, Catal was announced for the lineup in Tournament of Survival 8, alongside John Wayne Murdoch, Joey Janela, Sawyer Wreck, Ciclope, Toru Sugiura, Tomoya Hirata, Rina Yamashita, and Matt Tremont. When she's not wrestling in singles matches and taking over the professional landscape, she can be found tagging with Brandon Kirk, her husband. (Love the Kirks!)

How did you discover buffalo chicken egg rolls were your go-to dish?

I love an easy to make snack that is filling enough to pass as a stand alone meal. I absolutely hate cooking, especially on my days off, so this quick and savory meal quickly became a favorite of mine. A quick, easy, filling meal that can be modified to every taste bud and preference, and be a people pleaser at any get together. Plus, its super cheap to make.

In the recipe, you call for ranch for dipping, but if there was a battle of the dressings does ranch reign supreme over blue cheese?

RANCH FOREVER. I will absolutely die on this hill. You could bathe me in ranch and it still wouldn't be enough ranch for me. But, to each their own I guess

Is it a dish you whip out at a gathering to impress the guests?

I make this for my friends and family pretty often, although it's not really an impressive skill to stuff cheese and chicken into an egg roll! Hahaha, but people do appreciate and enjoy them.

You're on the road a lot. Is there ever a place or food in a town that's a must-have that gives you a taste of home?

I don't think much can make me feel like home like my mom's chicken cutlets do. I grew up with them, and although there is really nothing special about them physically, they bring me back to my childhood and I am absolutely a lady who loves nostalgia.

KASEY KIRK'S
CATAL BUFFALO CHICKEN EGGROLLS

SERVES: 10 PREP TIME: 15 MINUTES
TOTAL TIME: 40 MINUTES (25 IF YOU'RE SPEEDY)

INGREDIENTS NEEDED:

- EGG ROLL WRAPS
- OLIVE OIL
- 2 CUPS OF SHREDDED MOZZARELLA CHEESE
- 3.5 CUPS OF SHREDDED CHICKEN
- 4 OZ. CREAM CHEESE (OPTIONAL)
- 1/4 CUP BUFFALO SAUCE
- RANCH DRESSING FOR DIPPING

INSTRUCTIONS

1. COMBINE CHICKEN, CREAM CHEESE, BUFFALO SAUCE, AND MOZZARELLA IN A MEDIUM SIZED BOWL.

2. PLACE EGG ROLL WRAPPER IN A DIAMOND SHAPE. ADD A HEALTHY AMOUNT OF CHICKEN/CHEESE MIXTURE TO THE MIDDLE OF THE WRAPPER. FOLD UP THE MIDDLE OF THE WRAPPER, FOLLOWED BY TIGHTLY FOLDING IN THE SIDES. ROLL OPPISITE SIDE OVER TO IAKE COMPLETED EGG ROLL.

3. HEAT ABOUT A 1/2 IN. OF OIL IN A LARGE SKILLEt OVER MEDIUM HEAT. ONCE BUBBLING, ADD EGG ROLLS. FRY ABOUT ONE MINUTE ON EACH SIDE (UNTIL GOLDEN BROWN).

4. PLACE EGG ROLLS ON PAPER TOWEL LINED PLATE TO DRAIN EXCESS OIL AND COOL DOWN.

5. DIP IN RANCH AND GO TO TOWN!

PHOTO: RED SHOES MEDIA

RICKY ASADA

Texas based ring announcer and commentator Ricky Asada blends his wrestling career with his career as an award winning chef who has worked for big name restaurants in the San Antonio area.

Asada's name comes from his middle name, Richard, but also his grandfather who wrestled when he was young and also helped him get into wrestling. As for "Asada," well, it's the name of his favorite taco!

Asada has announced and commentated for companies like No Peace Underground, WrestleRave, Heavy Metal Wrestling, Uncanny Attractions, Borracho Pro, and Pale Pro Wrestling. He briefly broke into podcasting as well, which led to him working with Heavy Metal. Asada's fascination with commentary began with watching sports growing up.

Some of his favorite commentators include Harry Carey, Steve Stone, Bob Costas, Tony Schiavone, and Darrell Waltrip. Asada tells us that growing up, he and his brother Dave had a bit where they'd deliver commentary while they played Blitz and Madden. Soon enough, he found himself doing commentary for beer pong games at highschool parties.

RICKY ASADA'S
MICHELADA WINGS

INGREDIENTS NEEDED:

- A BOTTLE OF ZING ZANG
- LIME JUICE
- CILANTRO
- MAGGI SEASONING
- WORCESTERSHIRE
- VALENTINA BLACK LABEL
- 1 MODELO TALL BOY
- CELERY
- SALT & PEPPER
- TAJIN
- CHAMOY

INSTRUCTIONS

1. ADD ALL INGREDIENTS INTO A MEDIUM WALLED POT AND LET THEM REDUCE ON MEDIUM LOW HEAT. ADD HALF OF THE CILANTRO (YOU'RE JUST GONNA FISH IT OUT LATER). ADD CELERY LATER IF YOU WANT A CRUNCHIER CONSISTANCY.

2. FRY THE WINGS HOWEVER YOU WANT BUT I SUGGEST DOUBLE FRYING THEM. FIRST ON 300 FOR ABOUT 8-10 MINUTES THEN AFTER THEY SIT FOR A BIT CRANK THE HEAT TO 350 UNTIL SATISFIED.

3. SERVE SAUCE WARMED UP. TOSS YOUR WINGS, GARNISH WITH THE TAJIN AND A LIGHT DRIZZLE OF CHAMOY.

PHOTO BY MASON ENDRES

MICKIE KNUCKLES

Often regarded as the "Queen of Deathmatch" Mickie Knuckles is a pioneer in the hardcore wrestling scene, first debuting in 2003. First getting her start in IWA Mid-South in the early 2000s, Knuckles has since wrestled for companies like JCW, ICW No Holds Barred, WSU, OVW, CCW, and H2O. When she began her training, she would train five times a week, wrestle two, and still find time to maintain a job. She eventually began doing odds and ends like security, sound, refereeing, ring crew, and she worked concessions and gimmicks. Knuckles had also held various women's titles with combined reigns as the IWA Mid-South Women's Championship, the OVW Women's Championship, and Girl Fight Wrestling's Girl Fight Championship. Other titles held include the AWR Revolutionary Championship, DPW Champion, RPW Women's Championship, and the (now defunct) AIW Women's Championship.

Knuckles has also taken part in an extensive amount of tournaments throughout her career, including winning the aptly named Queen of the Death Matches in 2006, WSU's Queen and King of the Ring in 2014, CCW's Women's Tournament in 2017, the Death Becomes Her Female Deathmatch Tournament 2018, Girl Fight's 2020 Tournament, Insane Championship Wrestling's (ICW) Hardcore Death Match Challenge 2021, and Asylum Wrestling Revolutions' Goddess Of Death. Knuckles also competed in Tremont's Angels Of Death Tournament where she made it to the finals, wrestling Sawyer Wreck and Kennedi Copeland. In 2021, for the first time in her career, the hardcore legend placed on the PWI 500 at #390, #384 in 2022, and #111 on Bell to Belle's Women's 500 in 2023.

MICKIE KNUCKLE'S
STUFFED MUSHROOMS
INGREDIENTS NEEDED:

- 2 LARGE CONTAINERS OF PORTOBELLO MUSHROOMS (STEMS REMOVED & CAVITY CLEANED)
- 8 OZ. CREAM CHEESE
- 1 CUP OF CHEDDAR CHEESE
- 1/4 CUP OF GRATED PARMESAN
- 2 TSP OF BLACK PEPPER
- 2 TSP OF ONION POWDER
- 2 TB OF DANOS SEASONING (ORIGINAL OR SPICY)
- 1 TB OF VEGETABLE OIL
- 1 TB MINCED GARLIC

INSTRUCTIONS

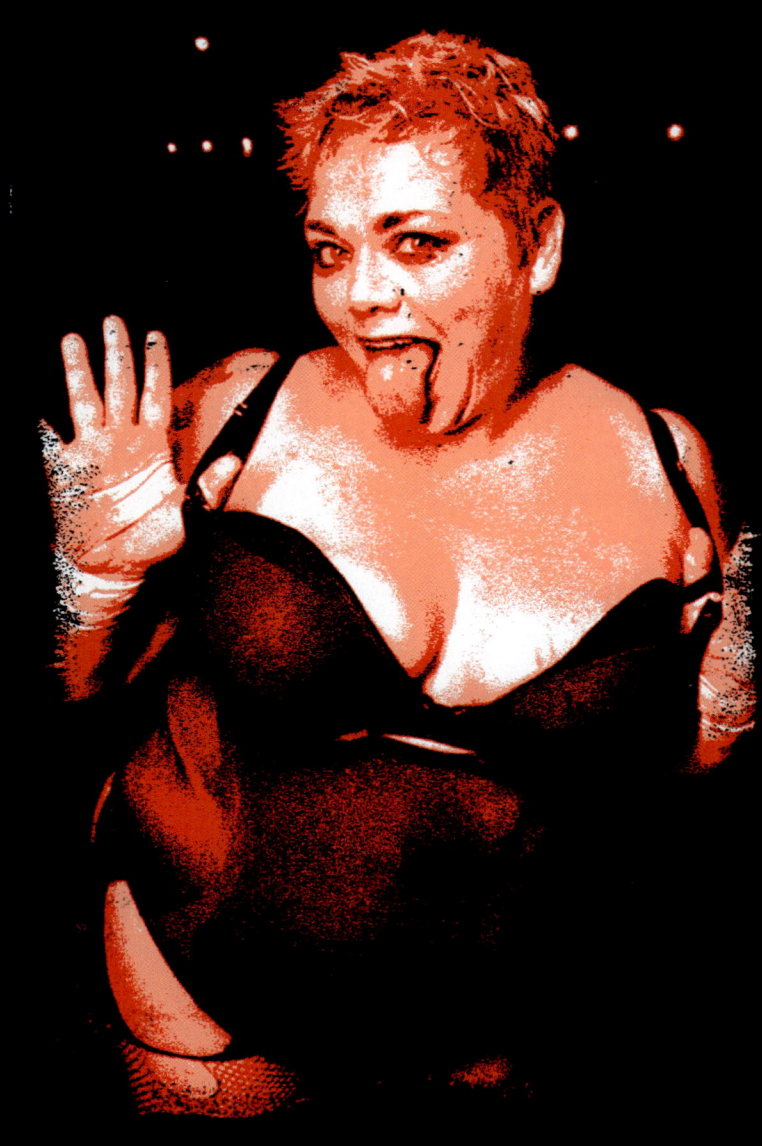

1. PREHEAT OVEN TO 350 F (175° C)

2. HEAT OIL AND MINCED GARLIC ON MEDIUM HIGH HEAT. COMBINE GROUND BEEF & ITALIAN SAUSAGE IN A LARGE SKILLET. GENEROUSLY SEASON WITH SALT & PEPPER AND COOK THOROUGHLY.

3. DRAIN MEAT, COMBINE BEEF/SAUSAGE, CREAM CHEESE, CHEDDAR CHEESE, ONION POWDER, BLACK PEPPER, AND DANOS SEASONING IN A LARGE BOWL.

4. CLEAN AND REMOVE MUSHROOM STEMS. TAKE A SMALL SPOON AND CAREFULLY REMOVE ALL REMAINING STEMS ON THE MUSHROOM CAPS. PAT DRY WITH A PAPER TOWEL TO REMOVE EXCESS MOISTURE.

5. USE A SMALL SPOON TO FILL IN EACH CAP GENEROUSLY. ARRANGE MUSHROOMS ON A COOKIE SHEET.

6. BAKE IN A PREHEATED OVEN FOR 20-25 MINUTES.

ANGEL METRO

Angel Metro is a fairly fresh face in wrestling, having graduated from the BWC Pro Wrestling Academy in 2022. Metro trained under Mike Mars, "The Broken Doll" Roxy, and BitDon. Based out of Virginia, she's wrestled up and down south and the midwest including in Tennessee, Florida, Ohio, Virginia, and New Jersey and she's the current BWC Cruiserweight Champion. Prior to training to become a wrestler, Metro was a musician, having worked in the goth/alternative scene for years. She categorizes her music as "dark electronic with bloodlines in synth pop and witch house."

"The Mistress of Fear" has wrestled for NPU, SSW, XCF, RCW, SWF, Asylum Carnage Wrestling, and ACW. Some of her favorite wrestlers growing up include Rey Mysterio, Chyna, Jake the Snake, and DDP which shows in Metro's style of wrestling – she's a smaller brawler but she uses her stature to her advantage with her agility.

ANGEL METRO'S
STUFFED JALAPEÑOS

INGREDIENTS NEEDED:

- 10 LARGE JALAPEÑOS
- 8 OZ. CREAM CHEESE SOFTENED
- 1/2 TSP GARLIC POWDER
- 1/2 TSP SALT
- 1/4 TSP PEPPER
- 1 1/2 CUP OF SHREDDED CHEDDAR CHEESE
- 1/2 LB VEGGIE SAUSAGE CRUMBLES

INSTRUCTIONS

1. PREHEAT OVEN TO 400°

2. SLICE EACH OF THE JALAPEÑOS IN HALF LENGTHWISE AND USE A SPOON TO CLEAN THE INSIDES OUT.

3. COMBINE THE CREAM CHEESE, GARLIC POWDER SALT, PEPPER, 1 CUP OF CHEDDAR, AND THE SAUSAGE CRUMBLES.

4. SPOON THE MIXTURE INTO THE JALAPEÑOS AND PLACE THEM ON A BAKING SHEET. TOP THE WITH THE REMAINING CHEDDAR.

5. BAKE FOR 20 MINUTES OR UNTIL JALAPEÑOS ARE TENDER.

PHOTO BY TUSSLEMANIA

JEFF CANNONBALL

Jeff Cannonball is a hardcore/deathmatch wrestler from New Jersey. Very early on in his career he put his name in the hat of hardcore, wrestling for the defunct NWS, OPW, and RTF, as well as FWF, and JCW before gaining notoriety in CZW. Cannonball has also wrestled numerous times for GCW, including in the Nick Gage Invitational where he defeated KTB in a first round matchup only to succumb to the late great Danny Havoc in the semi-final round. "The Deathmatch Vegan" is a two-time H2O Heavyweight champion and H2O Tag Team champion with Mitch Vallen as The Lone Rangers.

Cannonball was also a holder of H2O's Danny Havoc Hardcore Championship and the ISDub Falls Count Anywhere Championship. Cannonball is also a winner of OPW's Survival of the Sickest 2 tournament. When it comes to tag team wrestling, Cannonball has had his fair share of teams over the years, including with his wife, Terra Calaway, with Brandon Kirk as Rogues/Free to Think, with Kit Cannonball as the Cannonball Brothers, Matt Tremont as Weapons of Mass Destruction, and Puf as Club Soda.

JEFF CANNONBALL'S
VEGAN MINI MEATLOAFS
INGREDIENTS NEEDED:

- 1 PACKAGE OF "STOVE TOP" STUFFING MIX. THE ONE THAT SAYS FOR PORK (ITS VEGAN!)
- 1 CUP OF WATER
- 2 TB BBQ SAUCE
- 1 TB YELLOW MUSTARD
- 1 TB KETCHUP
- 1 TB GARLIC POWDER
- 1 LB BEYOND BEEF (IMPOSSIBLE WILL WORK TOO)
- SHREDDED VEGAN CHEDDAR CHEESE

INSTRUCTIONS

1. PREHEAT OVEN TO 375°.

2. COMBINE STUFFING MIX, WATER, BBQ SAUCE, KETCHUP, MUSTARD, AND GARLIC INTO A BOWL.

3. ADD THE FAKE BEEF IN AT THE END AND MIX IT THOROUGHLY. DIVIDE THE MIXTURE INTO A MUFFIN TIN.
(THIS WILL FILL 6 MUFFIN CUPS ABOUT 1 CUP PER CUP)

4. BAKE FOR 20 MINUTES. REMOVE AND TOP EACH LOAF WITH SHREDDED VEGAN CHEDDAR CHEESE (JUST A PINCH) AND BAKE FOR 3-4 MINUTES.

18.

PHOTO BY EARL GARDNER

LINDSAY SNOW

Based out of Jacksonville, Florida, Lindsay Snow holds many hats. A professional wrestler, women's champion, Bloodsport champion, and a tattoo artist, with a background in Brazilian jiu-jitsu, Snow's creative abilities are second to none. Training under veteran wrestler Jay Lethal, Snow debuted in 2016 and just a year later was afforded a WWE tryout opportunity at the Performance Center. At the time of writing, she has held titles in Full Throttle Pro Wrestling (FTPW) and IWE and is continuing to wrestle for titles all around the country. With an aspiration to go to Japan, Snow looked up to Japanese mixed martial artist and pro wrestler Kazushi Sakuraba growing up. In 2022, Snow landed in at #75 on the QWI ranking.

Decked out head-to-toe in tattoos, Snow's uniqueness doesn't stop at her appearance. In the ring, she can be seen mixing it up in all sorts of matches – No Ring Death, tag team, scrambles, hardcore, Deathmatches, standard singles matches – she's making a name for herself all throughout the independents. Snow has wrestled in companies like GCW (where she became a Bloodsport champion after beating Allysin Kay at Bloodsport 3), No Peace Underground (NPU), MPW, JCW, SHINE, and even AEW where she competed in Dark matches. A brutal striker and mat technician, the world belongs to Lindsay Snow.

LINDSAY SNOW'S
SNACKING BACON PUFF PASTRY

INGREDIENTS NEEDED:

- 1 LB. BACON
- 1 PKG OF PILLSBURY CRESCENT ROLLS
- 1/4 CUP MAPLE SYRUP
- 3/4 CUP BROWN SUGAR

INSTRUCTIONS

1. PREHEAT OVEN TO 375°.

2. LINE A BAKING SHEET (WITH RIM) WITH PARCHMENT PAPER AND LIGHTLY GREASE.

3. UNROLL CRESCENT ROLLS ONTO ONE FLAT PIECE AND PINCH THE PERFORATIONS TOGETHER AND STRETCH THE DOUGH TO FIT THE PAN AND PRICK THE DOUGH WITH A FORK.

4. CUT THE BACON INTO SMALL PIECES AND FRY THEM UNTIL THEY'RE JUST ABOUT DONE AND PLACE THEM ON A PAPER TOWEL TO DRAIN THE GREASE.

5. DRIZZLE HALF OF THE MAPLE SYRUP OVER THE CRESCENT DOUGH THEN SPRINKLE A LITTLE MORE THAN HALF OF THE BROWN SUGAR OVER THAT.

6. TOP THE DOUGH WITH BACON PIECES THEN ADD THE REST OF THE SYRUP AND BROWN SUGAR ON TOP OF THAT.

7. BAKE FOR 20-25 MINUTES OR UNTIL CARAMELIZED.

PHOTO BY CHRIS GRASSO

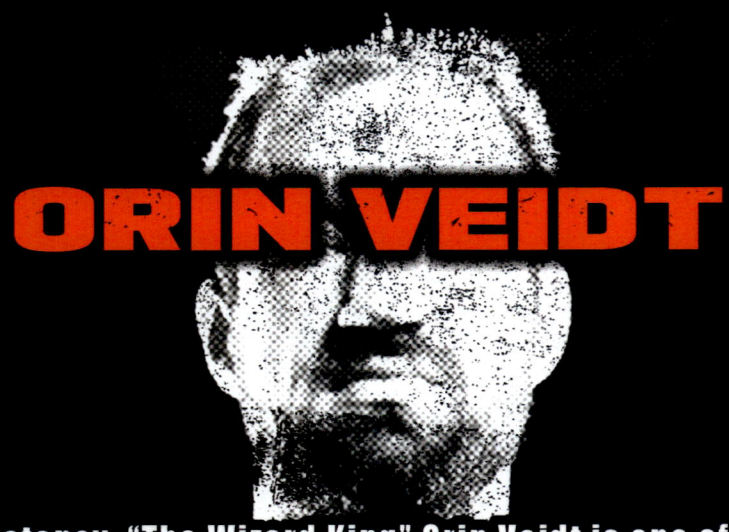

ORIN VEIDT

In terms of consistency, "The Wizard King" Orin Veidt is one of the most consistent Deathmatch wrestlers on the circuit. Starting his career in 2015, Veidt has wrestled for ICW No Holds Barred, IWA Mid-South, GCW, ICW (Insane Championship Wrestling), Rocky Mountain Pro, and CZW. Veidt is also a multi-time champion that got his start on the west coast and Canadian scene before heading to the Midwest and becoming a two-time ICW World and Alternative Champion, an Unsanctioned Pro Hardcore Champion, a Timebomb Champion, and an RMP Twitch Champion. Competing in tournaments and championship matches all around the United States, Veidt has defended his titles against some of the most beloved names in wrestling like AKIRA, Alex Colon, Matt Tremont, and Nick Gage, to name a few. Veidt has also done stints around the world including Japan where he competed in GCW and FREEDOMS as well as Mexico for DTU.

Veidt started his career as "The Dark Prophet," leaning into a "darker" side, popularized by wrestlers like Kane, The Undertaker, and The Ministry. After realizing that it wasn't working and something was missing, he shifted to "The Wizard King," heavily inspired by his love of anime and Black Clover.

ORIN VEIDT'S
SHRIMP ALFREDO ZUCCHINI BOATS
INGREDIENTS NEEDED:

- 4 LARGE ZUCCHINI, HALFED LENGTHWISE
- 1 TBSP. EXTRA VIRGIN OLIVE OIL
- 1 TSP. FRESH THYME LEAVES
- 2 TBSP. BUTTER
- 3/4 LB. LARGE SHRIMP, PEELED AND DEVEINED
- 2 TOMATOES, CHOPPED
- 3 CLOVES GARLIC, MINCED
- 1/4 C. HEAVY CREAM
- 1/4 C. FRESHLY GRATED PARMESAN
- 1/4 C. SHREDDED MOZZARELLA

INSTRUCTIONS

1. PREHEAT OVEN TO 350°. CUT ZUCCHINI IN HALF AND SCOOP OUT INSIDES WITH A SMALL SPOON, LEAVING 1/4"- THICK BORDER INTACT. CHOP ZUCCHINI PULP AND SET ASIDE.

2. PLACE ZUCCHINI BOATS IN A LARGE BAKING DISH AND DRIZZLE ALL OVER WITH OIL. SEASON WITH SALT AND PEPPER AND SPRINKLE THYME ON TOP. BAKE UNTIL TENDER, ABOUT 20 MINUTES.

3. IN A LARGE SKILLET OVER MEDIUM HEAT, MELT BUTTER. ADD SHRIMP AND SEASON WITH SALT AND PEPPER. COOK UNTIL PINK AND COOKED THROUGH, 3 TO 4 MINUTES. REMOVE FROM HEAT, LET COOL, THEN CHOP INTO BITE- SIZE PIECES.

4. RETURN SKILLET TO MEDIUM HEAT AND MELT REMAINING 1 TBSP BUTTER. ADD RESERVED ZUCCHINI PULP, TOMATOES, AND GARLIC, SEASON WITH SALT AND PEPPER, COOK UNTIL FRAGRANT, 1 MINUTE MORE. ADD CREAM, PARMESAN, AND COOK UNTIL SLIGHTLY REDUCED, 3 MINUTES. REMOVE FROM HEAT AND MIX IN COOKED SHRIMP.

5. FILL ZUCCHINI BOATS WITH SHRIMP MIXTURE AND TOP WITH MOZZARELLA.

GEORGE GATTON

Syracuse, New York born wrestler George Gatton also known as "Trashman" began his in-ring career at the CZW Academy where he was trained by Drew Gulak. Gatton consistently wrestled for CZW from the years 2014-2016 and in 2018 he appeared for Tournament of Death 16 in a Four Corners of Pain match against Dan O'Hare, Jimmy Lloyd, and Kit Osbourne.

In 2019, Gatton competed in GCW for Joey Janela's Spring Break 3 in the iconic Greatest Clusterfuck match. Gatton returned in 2022 for Spring Break 6 in Dallas, Texas for WrestleMania/The Collective weekend. Gatton appeared in ISDub for the Sean Henderson International Food Fight Invitational, winning the championship. He's wrestled all over the United States as well as the UK and Spain, making appearances in RCW, RWP, and ISW, among other promotions.

GEORGE GATTON'S
HAWAII CHIVE-O AND SAMMY
INGREDIENTS NEEDED:

- 3 LARGE EGGS
- 2 TBSP. CHIVE AND ONION CREAM CHEESE
- 1 TSP GROUND BLACK PEPPER
- 1 TSP SALT
- T TBSP UNSALTED BUTTER
- 2 SLICES OF SMOKED SALMON
- 1 HAWAIIAN BURGER ROLL

INSTRUCTIONS

1. WHISK 3 EGGS, SALT, AND PEPPER IN A BOWL,

2. MELT BUTTER IN A FRYING PAN OVER MEDIUM HEAT.

3. WHILE WAITING FOR BUTTER TO MELT, SPREAD 1 TBSP. OF CREAM CHEESE ON EACH BUN AND ADD 1 SLICE OF SMOKED SALMON TO EACH SIDE.

4. ADD EGG MIXTURE TO PAN, COOK FOR 2-3 MINUTES OVER MEDIUM HEAT, UNTIL DONE.

5. ADD EGGS TO BOTTOM BUN AND CONSTRUCT YOUR SANDWICH.

PHOTO BY EARL GARDNER

ZIGGY HAIM

If you've kept up with the independent scene in the last few years Ziggy Haim is a name that has taken over much of the Midwest as a professional wrestler, manager, and valet. Of Jewish ancestry, Haim has dominated the scene since 2017, becoming the Ryse Grand Champion, and as of this writing, is half of the current Enjoy Tag Team Champions with Derek Dillinger as The Production. They won the titles in a tag team tournament that saw some of the best teams on the independents compete, including Violence Is Forever, The Mane Event, BUSSY, Ephemeral Babes, and The Rip City Shooters, among others. Haim has also competed in Tremont's Angels of Death Tournament in a first-round Barbwire Brutality match against Sawyer Wreck. Haim is a mainstay in companies like AIW out of Cleveland, Ohio as well as Enjoy out of Pennsylvania, where she resides. So far in Haim's career, some of her match highlights include a Hair vs. Mask match against Edith Surreal at Enjoy Night Moves in 2021, and wrestling against the legendary Bill Alfonso in a Manager vs. Manager match at AIW's We Had A Few Hits A Few Years Ago. She was also ranked Pittsburgh City Paper's 2022 #3 Best Wrestler behind Kurt Angle and Lee Moriarty. Haim has also ranked in the PWI 500 at #403 in 2021 and #438 in 2022. Haim also ranked #31 in Outsports QWI (Queer Wrestling Index) in 2021 and #38 in 2022. "The Final Girl" is far from taking her final bow,

ZIGGY HAIM'S
CLASSIC NOODLE KUGEL

INGREDIENTS NEEDED:

- 16 OZ. WIDE EGG NOODLES
- 5 LARGE EGGS
- 1/2 C. BUTTER, MELTED
- 16 OZ. SOUR CREAM
- 8 OZ. COTTAGE CHEESE
- 3/4 C. GRANULATED SUGAR
- 1/2 TSP. CINNAMON

INSTRUCTIONS

1. PREHEAT OVEN TO 350° AND BUTTER A LARGE BAKING DISH

2. COOK THE NOODLES UNTIL AL DENTE (ABOUT 5 MINUTES, THEN DRAIN).

3. MIX THE REST OF THE INGREDIENTS TOGETHER IN A LARGE BOWL.

* IF YOU WANT A SILKY CONSISTENCY IN YOUR KUGEL, YOU CAN BLEND TOGETHER THE COTTAGE CHEESE AND SOUR CREAM BEFORE ADDING IT TO THE MIXING BOWL.

4. ONCE EVERYTHING IS MIXED, STIR THE NOODLES. POUR INTO THE BAKING DISH, AND BAKE UNTIL ITS SET (ABOUT 1 HOUR).

PHOTO BY EARL GARDNER

SEXXXY EDDY

Instead of abiding by the "don't try this at home" warnings, Canadian wrestler SeXXXy Eddy embraces them – and more. The veteran wrestler also known as "The Triple X Sex XXXpress" oozes sexual energy, I mean, he literally comes to the ring gyrating. What most would consider incredibly lewd, once Eddy is inside of the ring he captivates the audience all while wearing a g-string. Despite this, he's earned the respect of many of his peers, as many of them credit him for helping them break out onto the scene (WWE's Sami Zayn and Kevin Owens and AEW's Evil Uno). With over 20 years of experience, he's had his fair share of moments that have defined his career – perhaps most notably at CZW's Tournament of Death 3 – but even in the modern era, he's still making headlines and going viral, like when he wrestled Matt Cardona at GCW Worst Behavior and his trunks exploded (and he still hit the "naked" moonsault he's become synonymous with!)

Eddy is a multi-time champion with titles that include the ISW Falls Count Anywhere championship, and the IWS World Heavyweight championship. Eddy has also held the CZW Tag Team and Junior Heavyweight championship. He continues to wrestle consistently across Canada, including in ISDub, CWE, C4, and GPW, among many others.

SEXXXY EDDY'S
5 WAY SHEPHARDS PIE
INGREDIENTS NEEDED:

LAYER 1
- 2 LBS. OF DESIRED MEAT OR 3 CANS OF LENTILS

LAYER 2
- 1 CAN OF CORN KERNELS
- 1 CAN OF CREAM CORN

LAYER 3
- MUSHROOMS, PEPPERS, ONIONS, AND CANNED PEAS

LAYER 4
- 4 POTATOES
- 1 SWEET POTATO
- 2 CARROTS
- FRESH GARLIC/ GARLIC POWDER
- MILK
- BUTTER

LAYER 5
- GRATED MOZZARELLA OR CHEDDAR CHEESE

INSTRUCTIONS

LAYER 1: IN A LARGE PAN ON MEDIUM HEAT, BROWN, AND SEASON WITH STEAK SPICE AFTERWARDS. STIR ON HIGH HEAT UNTIL THE WATER EVAPORATES OR DRAIN IT.

LAYER 2: MIX THE CANS OF CORN KERNELS AND CREAM CORN AND SPREAD IT ALL OVER YOUR MEAT

LAYER 3: LOW-MED HEAT TO FRY AND CARAMELIZE THE ONIONS, MUSHROOMS, AND PEPPERS.

LAYER 4: I PREFER TO KEEP THE POTATO SKIN ON, BUT PEEL THEM IF YOU PREFER. CHOP, BOIL, DRAIN THEN MASH ALL TOGETHER. ADD SOME FRESH GARLIC OR GARLIC POWDER FOR TASTE. ADD BUTTER AND MILK.

BAKE AT 400 FOR 20 MINUTES, KEEPING AN EYE ON THE CHEESE UNTIL GOLDEN.

LET IT COOL FOR 10 MINUTES AND IT CAN BE CUT AND SERVED!

PHOTO BY SEXXXY EDDY

KEVIN GILL

Commentators are the voices behind every wrestling match that make some of the most surreal moments even more special. Kevin Gill, the voice behind many matches in GCW, is one of those people. Gill began his wrestling career as a referee in 2005 for Juggalo Championship Wrestling before commentating for Fire Pro TV and in 2009 joined the JCW commentary team where his play-by-play career would take off. From there, he would work shows in companies like Hoodslam, GRPW, West Coast Pro, ROL, Pandemonium: Pro Wrestling, Circle 6, and GCW. In 2018, Gill commented on Joey Janela's Spring Break 2, and from there, would be consistently featured on their programming for over four years. Gill has commentated on shows like GCW Tournament of Survival 666, Cage of Survival, The Art of War Games, GCW Fight Club 2021, Homecoming Weekend 2022, Effy's Big Gay Brunch, The Settlement Series, and more.

Outside of professional wrestling, Gill spent his formative years obsessed with music and video games as well, leading him to establish his own independent record label in the 90s, Striving For Togetherness Records. In the early 2000s, Gill designed two wrestling video games that also released critically acclaimed soundtracks of over 100 songs across both games. In 2013, Gill was cast as himself in Saints Row IV, the action-adventure game developed by Deep Silver: Volition and published by Deep Silver. He's also a successful podcaster, launching his own show with his namesake that was dubbed a "part of the golden age of podcasts" by Rolling Stone. Just like his social media handles suggest, Kevin Gill is the OG.

KEVIN GILL'S
POWERBOMB PASTA WITH VEGGIE MELEE
INGREDIENTS NEEDED:

- 1/2 CUP OF VIRGIN OLIVE OIL
- 6-8 CLOVES OF GARLIC MINCED OR 2 TSP OF GARLIC POWDER
- 2 TSP DRIED BASIL
- 2 TSP CRUSHED RED PEPPPER FLAKES
- 1/2 CUP SUN DRIED TOMATOES CHOPPED FIRMLY
- 2 CUPS VEGGIE BROTH
- 1/2 CUP WHITE WINE (I RECOMMEND CHARDONNAY)
- 2 CUPS PARMESAN CHEESE
- 6 CUPS OF BROCCOLI FLORETS
- 2 LARGE BELL PEPPERS (CHOPPED OR CHUNKS)
- SALT & PEPPER

INSTRUCTIONS

1. COOK PASTA ACCORDING TO PACKAGE DIRECTIONS.

2. PREHEAT OVEN TO 350 AND DRIZZLE OLIVE OIL AND BLACK PEPPER OVER BROCCOLI AND BAKE FOR 15 MINUTES.

3. DRAIN PASTA AND SIT ASIDE.

4. HEAT THE OLIVE OIL OVER A MEDIUM FLAME FOR A MINUTE OR TWO IN THE POT YOU JUST DRAINED.

5. ADD BLACK PEPPER, RED PEPPER FLAKES, AND BELL PEPPERS. SAUTEE OVER MEDIUM FOR 6-8 MINUTES STIRRING OCCASIONALLY.

6. ADD GARLIC, BASIL, SUN-DRIED TOMATOES FOR THE FINAL 2 MINUTES

7. ADD WINE AND COOK UNTIL THE AMOUNT OF WINE IS REDUCED BY HALF THEN ADD YOUR VEGGIE BROTH

8. ADD THE BROCCOLI AND PASTA AND STIR UNTIL HOT. ADD CHEESE AND SEASON WITH SALT & PEPPER.

9. GARNISH WITH A SPRINKLE OF MOZZARELLA AND RED PEPPER FLAKES

PHOTO BY EARL GARDNER

MASHA SLAMOVICH

Beginning her in-ring career in 2016, in the time since, Masha Slamovich has built an extensive resume for herself. Slamovich started her career in Japan with REINA, WAVE, and World Woman Pro-Wrestling Diana before conquering the United States and Canada. Slamovich, from Moscow, Russia has amassed an incredible nine title reigns including the West Coast Pro Wrestling Women's Championship, AAW Women's Championship, ETU Key To The East Championship, CFU Undisputed Championship, and the GCW World Championship, where she defeated Nick Gage for the title.

Some of her career highlights so far include wrestling women's wrestling icon Mickie James for the Impact Knockouts World Title, competing on AEW Dark in 2021, wrestling against Marina Shafir at Josh Barnett's Bloodsport 7, and wrestling Jordynne Grace in a Last Knockout Standing match for the women's championship at IMPACT's Bound for Glory 2022. Outside of singles titles and matches, Slamovich has delved into the tag team circuit with AKIRA (dubbed AVD), wrestling against the legendary team of Los Macizos, Bird Law (Mike Bailey and Veda Scott), and the Prize City Hooligans (Alec Price and B3CCA). Trained by Amazing Red, Chigusa Nagayo, Johnny Rodz, and Yusuke Kodama, Slamovich has earned the nickname "Russian Dynamite," exuding sheer power and strength no matter who she steps into the ring with.

MASHA SLAMOVICH'S
PLOV
INGREDIENTS NEEDED:

- 10 CHICKEN THIGHS
- SALT & PEPPER
- OLIVE OIL
- BABY CARROTS
- 1 SWEET ONION
- RICE
- WATER

INSTRUCTIONS

1. ADD 2 CUPS OF RICE AND WATER TO A BIG POT AND LET IT COOK

2. BOIL 10 CHICKEN THIGHS IN A SEPERATE POT UNTIL COOKED.

3. ADD SALT TO THE COOKING CHICKEN AND DICE THE BABY CARROTS AND ONIONS.

4. ADD SOME OLIVE OIL INTO A PAN AND GENTLY FRY THE ONIONS THEN ADD THE COOKED RICE AND CARROTS AND LET THEM COOK FOR A BIT.

5. PREHEAT THE OVEN TO 450 AND TAKE A LARGE BAKING SHEET AND ADD THE RICE MIXTURE TO IT. LINE THE CHICKEN THIGHS UP ON TOP OF IT AND ADD SALT AND PEPPER.

6. POUR ENOUGH BROTH FROM THE CHICKEN THIGHS ON TOP OF IT AND ADD SALT AND PEPPER.

7. BAKE FOR 35-40 MINUTES. ONCE THE RICE HAS RISEN ABOVE THE BROTH IT IS READY.

PHOTO BY CHRIS GRASSO

SAVAGE GENTLEMAN VICTOR BENJAMIN

Victor Benjamin, "The Real Savage Gentleman," began his in-ring career in 2016 under the ring name Shane InYaFace and he quickly began wrestling for International Wrestling Cartel (IWC), Greektown Pro Wrestling (GPW) out of Toronto, Canada, and IWA Mid-South. Since, he's wrestled in Beyond Wrestling, AIW, ROH, WrestlePro, Warrior Wrestling, FIGHTT Pro, NWA, AEW on AEW: Dark Elevation, and in GCW at Josh Barnett's Bloodsport 6 against Bad Dude Tito. Benjamin is a former ACW Heavyweight Champion (defunct) and Catalyst Wrestling Freestyle champion. Benjamin is also one half of Pretty Proper with Lady Frost, his wife.

As a big proponent of all things peanut butter, naturally, Benjamin is the leader of the Peanut Butter Platoon, his fanbase, which is also the name of his peanut butter with Fokken Nuts. Before transitioning to wrestling from combat, he was undefeated in MMA, having won multiple medals with a 3-0 pro career. He's also the holder of the custom Butterfinger championship that was crafted out of a social media prank.

SAVAGE GENTLEMAN VICTOR BENJAMIN'S
P.B BACON WRAPPED BURGER
INGREDIENTS NEEDED:

- GROUND BEEF (85/15 RECOMMENDED)
- SALT
- BLACK PEPPER
- CHEDDAR CHEESE (OPTIONAL)
- BACON (4-6 STRIPS PER BURGER)
- FOKKEN NUTS PEANUT BUTTER
- JALAPEÑO PEPPER JELLY
- PRETZEL BURGER BUNS OR GLAZED DONUTS

INSTRUCTIONS

1. MIX GROUND BEEF WITH SEASONING AND DICED ONION IN A LARGE BOWL AND FORM THE PATTY

2. STUFF THE PATTY WITH CHEDDAR CHEESE AND THEN WRAP IT IN BACON USING THE WEAVE TECHNIQUE.(SECURE WITH TOOTHPICKS IF YOU NEED)

3. PREHEAT YOUR GRILL TO 300-350 F AND PLACE THE PATTIES ON THE GRILL FOR 10 MINUTES WITH THE LID CLOSED.

4. AFTER 10 MINUTES FLIP THE BURGERS AND CLOSE THE LID AGAIN AND GRILL FOR ANOTHER 10 MINUTES UNTIL COOKED TO YOUR LIKING.

5. SLICE YOUR BUN (OR DONUT) IN HALF. ADD PEANUT BUTTER ON ONE SIDE AND PEPPER JELLY ON THE OTHER

6. LET YOUR BURGER SIT FOR 5 MINUTES THEN ENJOY

PHOTO BY AJ MILLER

CAMILLA LEWIS

Camilla Lewis, owner of Simon Babycat Soap Co., has been a wrestling fan since she was a kid. Growing up, she'd watch WWF with her older brother and she really gravitated toward Mean Gene Okerlund. In recent years, like many other wrestling fans, she's taken a liking to popular independent promotion GCW which introduced her to Deathmatch. In an interview conducted for Eating The Indies, Lewis discussed her passion for Deathmatch wrestling. "Deathmatch seemed to really speak to me because as an artist, I study materials. I was impressed with how much the wrestlers put their bodies and minds through for the fans. I think I also like the crashing of tubes, glass and doors. I went to school for art for years and we learned how to put things together, but in this medium? it's all about how it smashes to the ground!"

After viewing wrestling through the lens of a fan, Lewis decided to take a different approach and made a line of wrestling related soaps for wrestlers in GCW which led to her releasing a line through Simon Babycat Soap Co., which she founded in 2016. Through this venture, she's been able to sponsor various promotions, shows, and wrestlers with the help of the independent scene's most promising photographers. Some of her sponsorships include Guanatos Hardcore Crew, Interspecies Wrestling, GCW, Fight Forever, The Collective, No Peace Underground, Unsanctioned Pro, Dropkick Depression, ICW/Boardwalk Budz (Cannabis Cup), Kasey Catal, Mickie Knuckles, Matthew Justice, and Orin Veidt. But outside of wrestling? Lewis thanks her mother who worked as a confectioner when Lewis was young for her passion for cooking. Some of Lewis' favorite promotions and wrestlers include Kasey Catal, Rina Yamashita, Masha Slamovich, Lufisto, Sawyer Wreck, Mickie Knuckles, Edith Surreal, ICW, H20, and GCW.

When did your passion for cooking begin?

My mother was a confectioner when I was very little, around the age of five. She would have icing roses drying out on wax paper in the dining room. She would help with making cakes with beautiful icing around the church as my dad was a Methodist minister growing up.She got really good at many different types of cuisine, she would watch so many cooking shows, go to conventions,and collect cookbooks for as long as I can remember. Her creativity poured through her medium of cooking and for that I'm grateful. She was humble, loving, kind and the love of food probably started with her. She was an artist in icing, and creations. She conquered a lot by the time she passed in 2006. God blessed me with a lot, especially her.

What about cooking do you love the most?

Getting to try new flavors/cuisines from different cultures, the comradery and conversation over a meal you helped create, etc.?
 I think it's the passion about the contrast of flavor profiles. A couple of years ago, I learned about squeezing lime on dishes to bring out flavors but at the same time not adding salt or fat. There's also so many countries and types of cuisine that I haven't explored yet. I was a server for many years, and I was blessed to meet many chefs and I watched what they created and how they created it. The restaurant business is an invaluable resource, from the kitchen to the dining room. One thing I learned from them is to use local fresh ingredients during the height of their freshness to create different flavors for a wonderful meal. You can learn a lot by watching others who know their craft.

CAMILLA LEWIS'
MARYLAND CRAB SALAD AND CROSTINI
INGREDIENTS NEEDED:

- EQUAL PARTS CRAB MEAT(CLAW & LUMP 1/2 LB EACH)
- 1/2 CUP DUKS MAYONNAISE
- 1/2 LEMON
- 1 TSP. OLD BAY SEASONING

INSTRUCTIONS

1.GENTLY SIFT THROUGH THE CRAB MEAT TO REMOVE ANY SHELLS.

2.GENTLY PLACE IN A BOWL WITH MAYONNAISE, LEMON JUICE, AND OLD BAY AND FOLD IT WITH A SPATULA.
SEASON.ADJUST MAYO TO TASTE

I LIKE TO PLACE THIS SALAD ON A BED ARUGULA SPINACH MIX WITH SHREDDED CARROTS, A FEW CAPERS, FRESH CHERRY TOMATOES, LEMON WEDGE, AND A SIDE OF PINE NUT HUMMUS

36.

PHOTO BY CAMILLA LEWIS

BAM SULLIVAN

In the hardcore and Deathmatch wrestling scene, Bam Sullivan a.k.a. "The Trash With The Stache" is one of the names that should be on everybody's radar. Since 2016, Sullivan has been quietly making a name for himself in the tri-state area with companies like H2O and JCW where he's a mainstay talent. Through these encounters, alongside appearances in GCW and ICW. Sullivan became the inaugural H2O Danny Havoc Hardcore Champion, holding the title for 168 days. Sullivan has also won the H2O tag team titles with Aidan Baal as The Extricated, the NYWC Fusion Championship, and he is a two-time NYWC tag team champion with Boo Sullivan as The Hounds of Hatred.

Sullivan has stepped into the ring with some of the most notable names in the hardcore/deathmatch arena, including Alex Colon, Lowlife Louie, Casanova Valentine, AKIRA, Sawyer Wreck, SHLAK, and John Wayne Murdoch. He appeared in IWA Mid-South for the 2021 edition of KOTDM (King of the Deathmatch) where he made it all the way to the quarter-finals in a three-way Wire Nets, Tubes, and Panes Deathmatch. Sullivan is also, in his own words, the "godfather [and] almighty creator of Clutch Your Nuts," a term coined as a spoof of the controversial wrestling promotion Control Your Narrative.

BAM SULLIVAN'S
BAMBURGER
INGREDIENTS NEEDED:

- 1/2 LB. GROUND BEEF PATTY (BUBBA BURGER BRAND)
- 1 SLICE OF AMERICAN CHEESE
- 3 STRIPS OF MAPLE BACON
- 1 FRIED EGG (PREFERABLY WITH A LITTLE RUNNY YOLK)
- LETTUCE
- TOMATO
- SESAME SEED BUN

INSTRUCTIONS

1. COOK THE PATTY IN A PAN WITH BUTTER UNTIL MEDIUM/RARE.

2. ADD A SLICE OF CHEESE AND LET IT MELT BEFORE ADDING THE PATTY TO YOUR BOTTOM BUN.

3. THROW AN EGG ON A SEPARATE PAN AND COOK IT UNTIL IT'S MOSTLY COOKED BUT EVER SO SLIGHTLY RUNNY.

4. FRY UP SOME BACON STRIPS UNTIL DESIRED AND ADD THEM TO THE PATTY. (I LIKE THIN CRISPY BACON, NOT BURNT)

5. ADD SLICED TOMATO AND SOME LETTUCE AND CALL IT A DAY.

PHOTO BY EARL GARNDER

MIKE "ROTCH" WOODS

Mike Woods (a.k.a. Mike Rotch) is the owner and promoter of independent wrestling promotion Interspecies Wrestling, a company that was founded in 2005 with the idea that all of the shows housed under its banner would be something fans have never seen before. They make wrestling for "people who don't like wrestling" by combining styles like technical, deathmatch, and the comedic style of wrestling and reinvent the way fans view the sport. The promotion has had an immense amount of star power walk through its doors, including WWE's Kevin Owens and Sami Zayn and AEW's Eddie Kingston, Stu Grayson, and Evil Uno, to name a few.

Over the years, ISW built a name for itself by utilizing a certain interlocking colored block toy (you know the one). In 2019, the company took part in GCW's Collective weekend and put on Boner Jam IV: Balls Out. The show saw the likes of The Butcher and Blade, Tony Deppen, a Falls Count Anywhere match between Sexxxy Eddy and Swoggle, and a colored block toy deathmatch with Matt Tremont defeating Jeff Cannonball, Nick Gage, and Addy Starr for the title. In 2021, they put on the Slamtasia 7: The Big Dumb Block Party after a two year hiatus. The event caught headlines for hosting a 1,000,000 Block Deathmatch at the H2O Center in Williamstown, New Jersey.

MIKE "ROTCH" WOODS'
CHICKPEA SALAD

INGREDIENTS NEEDED:

- 1 CAN OF CHICKPEAS - DRAINED
- 1 BUNCH OF FRESH PARSLEY - CHOPPED
- 1 LARGE CUCUMBER - CUT INTO LITTLE CUBES
- 1 LARGE TOMATO - DICED
- 1 RED BELL PEPPER - CHOPPED
- 1 MEDIUM SIZED RED ONION - DICED
- CRUMBLED FETA CHEESE
- OLIVE OIL
- LEMON JUICE
- SALT & PEPPER (OPTIONAL)

INSTRUCTIONS

1. THROW EVERYTHING INTO A BOWL

2. IN ANOTHER BOWL, MIX EQUAL PARTS OLIVE OIL AND LEMON JUICE. ADD SOME HONEY TO THAT. (I NEVER MEASURE I JUST GO UNTIL IT TASTES GOOD) THROW A LITTLE SALT AND PEPPER IN TOO. (IF YOU WANT)

3. POUR THE DRESSING INTO THE BOWL WITH THE OTHER INGREDIENTS, AND MIX IT ALL UP. MINGLE. LET EVERYONE GET TO KNOW EACH OTHER N' STUFF.

THEN EAT IT

40.

EFFY

When you look at the scope of independent wrestling, Effy's impact on the industry in such a short amount of time, including in the LGBTQ+ community, cannot be overlooked. Since creating Effy's Big Gay Brunch, he's garnered cheers and applause even in the most conservative towns. Effy is a multi-time champion, holding the FEST Wrestling championship twice, an AWE Tag Team champion, Freelance Legacy champion, Inspire Pure Pro Prestige champion, and a GCW Tag Team champion. Speaking of tag teams, Effy has been part of numerous tag teams including Effy Loves Beastly, Gaytanic Panic with Danhausen, EffyKat with Allie Kat (what would later become known as BUSSY with Allie Katch).

Effy has created many memorable moments in his career thus far, including wrestling Jeff Jarrett at The Wrld on GCW at the iconic Hammerstein Ballroom in New York City, wrestling Jon Moxley for the GCW World Title at GCW Homecoming 2022, becoming an entrant for TOS 666, becoming a semifinals participant in the ENJOY Cup: Tag Team Edition, and winning the Invitational Grand Prix Tournament Of Tournaments Classic International in 2020. In 2021 he created a brand that even the most "casual" wrestling fans have seen attending events or walking down the street: Wrestling Is Gay. The movement helps give back to causes helping combat rampant homophobia and discrimination while also reclaiming a word that was often used to demonize individuals. Outside of wrestling, Effy has worked on Dead End: Paranormal Park voicing the character Asmodeous. Effy knows he's a controversial personality, but isn't afraid to lean into it. Whether you love him or hate him, he doesn't shy away from being his authentic self because this is EFFY and he's here to stay.

EFFY'S
MISSIONARY CHRISTMAS STEAK & CREAM RICE
INGREDIENTS NEEDED:

STEAK

- 2 LB. ROUND STEAK
- 3 TBS FLOUR
- SALT
- 2 TBS OIL
- 1 6 OZ. CAN OF MUSHROOMS (DRAINED)
- TOMATO
- 1 CONTAINER OF SALSA.

CREAM RICE

- 1 C. COOKED RICE
- 2 C. SOUR CREAM
- GRATED JACK CHEESE
- 1 4 OZ. CAN OF GREEN CHILES

INSTRUCTIONS

STEAK

1.COMBINE FLOUR, SALT, AND PEPPER. DREDGE THE MEAT WITH THIS. BROWN THE MEAT IN A SKILLET WITH OIL BRIEFLY.PUT THE MEAT IN THE CROCKPOT AT 325 DEGREES WITH SALSA POURED OVER. COOK FOR 2 HOURS. ADD THE CANNED MUSHROOMS IN THE LAST 10 MINUTES OF COOKING.

CREAM RICE

1.COOK THE RICE AND MIX WITH SOUR CREAM. LAYER THE RICE WITH CHEESE AND THE CANNED PEPPERS TWICE. BAKE FOR 30 MINUTES AT 325.

2. PUT A BIG OLD SCOOP OF THAT CREAM RICE ON A PLATE THEN PUT STEAK AND SALSA ON TOP. EAT IT.

42.

PHOTO BY EARL GARDNER

BILLIE STARKZ

Billie Starkz made her professional wrestling debut in 2018 at 13 years old. Since then, Starkz has wrestled all over the world and is showing no signs of slowing down. Balancing going to school with her wrestling career, Starkz has been a mainstay in companies like BLP, where she won the Heavyweight Championship, and GCW. In 2022, at just 17 years old, Starkz made her debut in AEW against Britt Baker and in Japan with TJPW. She's heavily featured on Ring of Honor television and competed in her first televised title match against Jade Cargill for the TBS Championship and even pinned one of the industry's most respected veterans, Matt Tremont at the H2O Center. From 2022 to 2023 Starkz has wrestled some of the biggest names in the industry including Toni Storm, Maki Itoh, Miyu Yamashita, Yuka Sakazaki, Chelsea Green, Ruby Soho, Willow Nightingale, and BUSSY (Allie Katch and EFFY). You'd be hard-pressed to find a teenager with a more extensive resume.

At 18, Starkz is still focused on going to college and getting her degree while also pursuing her passion for professional wrestling. She's also the head of the Big Starkz Brand (BSB) with both of her parents. The brand, which originally started as a joke on Twitter, has amassed love from across the globe with everyone wanting to rep the BSB! Including the BLP Heavyweight title, Starkz has already collected six titles, including the CCW Global Fighting Championship, 2econd Wrestling Championship, Girl Fight Championship, H2O Hybrid Championship, and the PHW Party Monster Championship. (Billie the Belt Collector? We're all for it!) Whether she's Space Jesus, Young William, Billiam, the Blue Gremlin, or just Billie Starkz – she's taking over the world just like she's taking over Eating the Indies!

BILLIE STARKZ
EASY WHITE CHILI

INGREDIENTS NEEDED:

- 2 PACKETS OF MCCORMIK WHITE CHILI MIX
- 2 LBS. OF CHICKEN BREAST
- 1 SMALL ONION - DICED
- 2 CANS OF CORN - DRAINED
- 2 CANS OF NORTHERN BEANS
- 2 CUPS OF WATER

GARNISH OPTIONS:

- SOUR CREAM
- BANANA PEPPERS
- SHREDDED CHEESE (ANY)

INSTRUCTIONS

1. CUBE CHICKEN AND COOK ON STOVE WITH A SMALL AMOUNT OF OLIVE OIL UNTIL DONE.

2. WHILE IT COOKS DUMP EVERYTHING ELSE IN A SLOW COOKER AND STIR WELL.

3. ONCE CHICKEN IS FINISHED DRAIN ANY EXCESS OIL AND ADD CHICKEN TO SLOW COOKER AND STIR.

4. COOK ON LOW FOR 8 HOURS OR HIGH FOR 4 HOURS.

5. ADD TO A BOWL AND GARNISH WITH THE ABOVE ITEMS.

PHOTO BY EARL GARDNER

CASANOVA VALENTINE

New York based wrestler and part owner of New Fear City (NFC) Casanova Valentine otherwise known as the "King of the No Ring Deathmatch" is taking over the tri-state area of deathmatch wrestling. Valentine began his in ring career in 2014 for New York Wrestling Connection (NYWC) and Warriors Of Wrestling before ultimately starting his own promotion in 2016, "Death Match," which morphed into "No Ring Death Match," and then NFC, as it stands today.

Valentine has wrestled the likes of Matt Tremont, SHLAK, the late great Markus Crane, Louie Ramos, Big Joe, MJF, Nick Gage, Mance Warner, Effy, Akira, Atticus Cogar, and Cole Radrick, to name a few. Outside of his own promotion, Valentine can be seen in promotions like Circle 6, ICW No Holds Barred, RISE, and Unsanctioned Pro, where he defeated Cane to win the Unsanctioned Pro Hardcore Championship, his first of three reigns with the title.

Valentine has also held the RISE Hardcore championship, the RISE championship that he won in the "Games of Death" tournament, the NPU championship, and the defunct HMW Bexar Knuckles championship and NLW Deathmatch championship. Valentine has spearheaded the No Ring Death Match concept, of which he has wrestled in over 100 matches.

CASANOVA VALENTINE'S
BROOKLYN BLACK DEATH BANG BANG CHICKEN
INGREDIENTS NEEDED:

CRISPY CHICKEN

- 3 1 LB. CHICKEN BREASTS - CHOPPED INTO BITE SIZE CHUNKS.
- 3 TBSP. CORNFLOUR
- 1/2 C. BUTTERMILK
- 1 EGG
- 3/4 TSP. GARLIC SALT
- 1/4 TSP WHITE PEPPER
- 1 TSP. SALT
- 3 C. PANKO BREADCRUMBS
- 1 TSP. PAPRIKA
- 1/2 TSP. BLACK PEPPER
- 1/2 TSP. CELERT SALT
- 1/4 TSP. WHITE PEPPER
- 2 TBSP. OLIVE OIL

BANG BANG SAUCE

- 1/2 C. MAYONNAISE
- 2 TBSP. SWEET CHILI SAUCE
- 1 TBSP. SRIRACHA SAUCE.
- 1 TSP. HONEY

TO SERVE

- 4 SPRING ONIONS SCALLIONS - SLICED
- 1 RED CHILLI - THINLY SLICED

INSTRUCTIONS

1. PREHEAT THE OVEN TO 200C/400F.

2. START BY MAKING THE BANG BANG SAUCE. PLACE THE MAYONNAISE, SWEET CHILI SAUCE, SRIRACHA, AND HONEY IN A SMALL BOWL AND MIX TOGETHER THEN PUT TO THE SIDE.

3. PLACE THE CORNFLOUR IN ONE BOWL.

4. PLACE THE BUTTERMILK,EGG, 1/4 TSP.GARLIC SALT, 1/5 TSP. WHITE PEPPER AND 1/2 TSP. SALT IN A SECOND BOWL AND LIGHTLY WHISK TO COMBINE.

5. PLACE THE PANKO, PAPRIKA,1/2 TSP SALT, 1/2 TSP PEPPER, 1/2 TSP. GARLIXC SALT, 1/2 TSP. CELERY SALT, 1/4 TSP. WHITE PEPPER AND 2 TBSP. OLIVE OIL IN A THIRD BOWLAND MIX TOGETHER UNTIL THE OLIVE OIL IS COMBINED WITH THE BREADCRUMBS EVENLY.

6. DREDGE THE CHICKEN PIECES IN THE CORNFLOUR, THEN DIP THE BUTTERMILK MIXTURE TO COAT AND FINALLY COAT THE CHICKEN IN THE PANKO MIXTURE.

7. PLACE ON A BAKING TRAY AND PLACE THE BAKING TRAY IN THE OVEN AND COOK FOR 20 MINUTES, UNTIL THERES NO PINK IN THE MIDDLE THEN TRANSFER INTO A SERVING BOWL AND DRIZZLE OVER HALF IN SAUCE

8. SPRINKLE OVER THE SPRING ONIONS AND SLICED CHILLI, THEN SERVE WITH THE REMAINING BANG BANG SAUCE FOR DIPPING

46.

JIMMY DEACON

In professional wrestling, there are a lot of people that help keep the wheels turning behind the scenes. On the independent scene specifically, this rings true with ring crew, commentary, referees, etc. They're all committed to making the best possible product they can because their love and passion for professional wrestling far exceed anything else. One of those people is Jimmy Deacon, a wrestling fan turned referee inspired by the late great Sean Patrick O'Brien (SPO), a beloved referee on the independents that had a dedicated passion for the world of professional wrestling. Deacon first began his career doing ring crew for H2O, GCW, ICW: NHB, Bloodstorm Pro, and SHP (Sean Henderson Presents). Through this, it has given him the opportunity to travel and work locally in New Jersey. When Deacon became a referee, the first show he worked on was Undiscovered 66 for H2O, leading him to a televised match at Sean Henderson Presents: Candy Paint. But he's not finished yet. In fact, he's just getting started.

When did you discover your love for cooking?

I discovered my passion in September 2017. I had just quit my job at Amazon, one of my good friends in college had passed, and I was down on my luck. A friend of mine worked at a bar and asked if I wanted a job one day when I visited, I said yes. He asked if I could cook. I said, "I'm ready to learn." A month into the job at Wilson's Pub, I found a deep love for the culinary that I never knew I had that continues to this day.

How did you discover it was your favorite dish?

As a child, I was awfully picky and as a teenager, I struggled to change that. I had too many comfort foods I would eat instead of trying something new. Chicken Parmesan, as a platter and as a sandwich, was one of them. You know how people will say they can tell how good a place is based on their "wings" or "cheesesteaks?" The chicken parm sandwich is my litmus test of sorts. When I realized how much freedom I had to experiment in the kitchen, I immediately started working on making the best iteration of the sandwich I could, and even though it's always evolving, I think I found it.

Is it a dish you whip out at a gathering to impress the guests?

It's one of the top three I consider making when having a big gathering. I made it for a Friendsgiving years ago as a buffet-style serving. Cooked up a few pounds of chicken, put it in a large tin, and threw it in the oven. The pictures alone of it caused my friends' mouths to water.

Is it an original recipe or do you make any alterations or add-ons to make it uniquely yours?

So as previously mentioned, it's a heavily altered chicken parmesan sandwich that I've crafted to my tastes. You'll see Old Bay seasoning on the recipe list and while you may look at me crazy, I'm a huge Old Bay guy. Sometimes I throw Cajun on it. What my (Italian) friends really get on my case about is that I throw White American cheese on it. But The Deacon isn't the same without that two to three cheese ooze out of the roll.

JIMMY DEACON'S
THE DEACON
(MY TAKE ON A CHICKEN PARM SANDWICH)
INGREDIENTS NEEDED:

- -1 LARGE CHICKEN BREAST
- -AMERICAN CHEESE
- -MOZZARELLA CHEESE
- -SALT
- -PEPPER
- -OLD BAY
- -GARLIC POWDER
- -1 FOOT LONG ROLL
- -MARINARA

"THE SPIRIT OF THE SANDWICH IS THAT YOU'RE TAKING SOMETHING PRE-EXISTING, AND MAKING IT YOUR OWN. LIKE WRESTLERS MAKING THEIR FINISHER DIFFERENT WITH THEIR OWN FLAVOR. AS LONG AS YOU'RE HAPPY WITH THE END RESULT... YOU'VE MADE THE DEACON"

INSTRUCTIONS

1.TAKE YOUR CHICKEN BREAST AND BUTTERFLY IT INTO TWO PIECES. SEASON EACH SIDE TO PREFERENCE. WITH SALT, PEPPER, OLD BAY, GARLIC POWDER, AND ALL-PURPOSE SEASONING. ONCE SEASONED, BEGIN COOKING ON YOUR HEATED MEDIUM OF CHOICE

2.WHILE COOKING THE CHICKEN, YOU CAN PREP YOUR ROLL WITH A SLICE THROUGH THE MIDDLE LONGWAYS. FROM THERE YOU CAN TOAST IT IF YOU'D LIKE.

3.ONCE THE CHICKEN IS FULLY COOKED THROUGH, CHOP IT TO PREFERENCE, NOW, PLACE THREE TO FOUR SLICES OF AMERICAN CHEESE ATOP THE CHICKEN AND DRIZZLE SOME MARINARA SAUCE OVER TOP. ONCE MELTED, FLIP THE CHICKEN OVER ITSELF TO GET AS MUCH OF THE MELTED CHEESE ON IT.THEN REPEAT THIS STEP WITH MOZZARELLA.

4.ONCE MELTED YOU CAN START FILLING YOUR ROLL WITH YOUR HARD WORK AND ENJOY.

PHOTO BY JIMMY DEACON

BIG F'N JOE

When looking at the cornerstone of BritWres, Big F'n Joe cannot be overlooked. Beginning his wrestling career in 2005 as "Jo FX," he mainly wrestled for World Association of Wrestling (WAW), the defunct RDW and DAM. Over the course of his career up until 2010, Joe wrestled pretty consistently and took a few bookings in the years that followed. In the spring of 2016 he began wrestling for RISE Underground as a regularly featured talent.

In 2019, Joe made his way over the pond to Las Vegas, Nevada where he wrestled at New Fear City in a No Ring Death Match for the RISE title against Casanova Valentine and the late great Markus Crane. He would go on to unseat Valentine as champion. In the summer of that same year, Joe would wrestle in CZW's Tournament of Death 18 in New Jersey. Since, he's wrestled in the aforementioned promotions as well as TNT, LWP, and ICW No Holds Barred where he wrestled against Hoodfoot. Joe continues to wrestle all over the U.K. and the United States, even popping up in GCW between mid to late 2022.

Joe is a multi-time champion in RISE as the Champion, Hardcore Champion (a now defunct title), and the European Deathmatch Champion. Joe has also held the DOA Pandemonium championship, NHW Hardcore championship, KCW Death Wolf championship, and the DOA UK Tag Team championship with Danny Darko.

BIG F'N JOE'S
CHICKEN & MUSHROOM STEW (WITH DUMPLINGS)
INGREDIENTS NEEDED:

CHICKEN STEW

- 3 OZ. THICK BACON CUT INTO 2/4 PIECES
- 1/4 C. ALL PURPOSE FLOUR
- 2 CHICKEN QUARTERS (THIGH AND LEG)
- KOSHER SALT
- FRESHLY GROUND PEPPER
- 1/4 C. WHITE WINE (SAUVIGNON BLANC) OR WHITE WINE VINEGAR
- 1 LB. MINCED MUSHROOMS
- 1 MEDIUM ONION - CHOPPED
- 1 C. CARROTS - CHOPPED
- 2/3 C. FROZEN PEAS
- 1 LARGE STICK CELERY - DICED
- 2 TSP. WORCESTSHIRE SAUCE
- 1 TSP. CHICKEN BOUILLON BASE (OPTIONAL)
- 3 GARLIC CLOVES - CRUSHED
- 2 SPRIGS THYME
- 1/4 TSP. EACH: DRIED BASIL, THYME, MUSTARD POWDER, ONION POWDER,
- 1/4 TSP. GROUND SAGE
- 1 BAY LEAF
- 4-5 C. CHICKEN BROTH.

DUMPLINGS

- 2 C. CAKE FLOUR
- 2 TSP. BAKING POWDER
- 1/2 TSP. BAKING SODA
- 1 TSP. SALT
- 1/2 TSP. ONION POWDER
- 1/8 TSP. NUTMEG
- 2 TSP. SUGAR
- 3/4 C. COLD SOUR CREAM
- 1/4 C. MILK
- 4 TBSP. BUTTER - MELTED
- 2 TBSP. CHOOPPED FRSH PARSLEY (OPTIONAL)
- 1 TBSP. CHOPPED FRSSH CHIVES. (OPTIONAL)

INSTRUCTIONS

1. CRISP BACON IN A DUTCH OVEN OVER MEDIUM HEAT; TRANSFER TO A PAPER TOWEL LINED PLATE.

2. PLACE FLOUR IN A SHALLOW BOWL. SEASON CHICKEN WITH SALT AND PEPPER AND DREDGE IN FLOUR. WORKING IN BATCHES COOK CHICKEN SKIN SIDE DOWN TO SEAR IN THE SAME POT WITH BACON GREASE. OVER MEDIUM HEAT SEAR 3 MINUTES EACH SIDE, TAKE CHICKEN OUT, PLACE ON PLATE. (IT WILL FINISH COOKING IN STEW)

3. PLACE MUSHROOMS, SALT, AND PEPPER IN SAME POT STIRRING OCCASIONALLY, UNTIL BROWN, 5-8 MINUTES WITH WOODEN UTENSIL, TRANSFER TO A BOWL. ADD ONION, CELERY, CARROTS, AND GARLIC TO THE SAME POT STIRRING OCCASIONALLY, UNTIL ONION IS SOFT AND TRANSLUCENT, 5-8 MINUTES. SCRAPE UP ANY REMNANTS FROM THE BOTTOM OF THE POT AS YOU DO SO. (THIS IS WHERE THE FLAVORS BUILD.)

4. ADD WINE INTO ONIONS/GARLIC/WORCESTERSHIRE INTO A SMALL POT; ADD A TBSP. OF BUTTER, SIMMER UNTIL REDUCED BY HALF, ABOUT 5 MINUTES

5. ADD CHICKEN, BACON, ALL HERBS, BROTH, CHICKEN BOUILLON BASE (OPTIONAL) SEASON WITH SALT AND PEPPER. BRING TO A BOIL, REDUCE HEAT, AND GENTLY SIMMER ON STOVE, PARTIALLY COVERED, SKIMMING OCCASSIONALLY, UNTIL CHICKEN IS FALLING OFF THE BONE, AROUND 1 1/2 HOURS. ADD PEAS AND MUSHROOMS AND SIMMER UNTIL FLAVORS MELD, 10- 15 MINUTES; SEASON WITH SALT & PEPPERAS NEEDED.

6. COMBINE THE FLOUR, BAKING POWDER, BAKING SODA, SALT, ONION POWDER, SUGAR, AND HERBS IN A MEDIUM BOWL, ADD THE MILK, SOUR CREAM AND MELTED BUTTER. USE A FOLDING MOTION TO COMBINE AND FORM A DOUGH, BUT DONT OVERMIX.

7. USE A SMALL SPOON AND CAREFULLY PLACE THE DUMPLINGS OVER THE SOUP IN AN EVEN LAYER. SPOON A LITTLE LIQUID OVER EACH ONE. COVER TIGHTLY AND INCREASE HEAT SLIGHTLY TO BRING IT TO A GENTLY SIMMER. SET A TIME FOR 15 MINS, DON'T LIFT THE LID DURING THIS TIME, THE DUMPLINGS NEED TO STEAM.

8. OPEN THE LID AND INSERT A TOOTPICK TO CHECK IF THE DUMPLINGS ARE DONE. ONCE THE MIDDLE IS SET, GARNISH WITH PARSLEY AND SERVE!

JOEY SILVER

"Sweet Cheeks" Joey Silver may appear as sweet as can be, but when it's time to get into the ring, he's anything but! As of this writing, Silver has held titles in House of Glory and Full Faith Wrestling. He continues to be a dominant (but nevertheless, sweet!) force in professional wrestling. After wrestling consistently from 2013-2015, Silver stepped away from wrestling but came back more determined than ever.

Throughout the pandemic era of wrestling, Silver trained at The Nightmare Factory and appeared in RPW, Synergy, NYWC, and even on episodes of AEW Dark against Michael Nakazawa, The Gunn Club, and The Dark Order. Silver also teamed with Kip Steven as Nerd World Order on the independents for a bit of time and HOGPD with Evander James and Scarlett Meidan.

JOEY SILVER'S
SWEET CHEEKS' FAMOUS DELECTABLE BLONDIES

INGREDIENTS NEEDED:

- 3/4 C. BUTTER, MELTED
- 1 C. LIGHT BROWN SUGAR.
- 1/2 C. GRANULATED SUGAR
- 2 EGGS
- 1 TBSP. VANILLA EXTRACT
- 1/2 TSP. SALT
- 1 3/4 C. ALL PURPOSE FLOUR
- 1/2 C. CHOPPED DARK CHOCOLATE

INSTRUCTIONS

1. PREHEAT OVEN TO 350F AND LINE A 8X8 BAKING PAN WITH PARCHMENT PAPER. LEAVE PARCHMENT PAPER HANGING OVER THE SIDES OF THE PAN SO THAT YOU CAN EASILY REMOVE THE BLONDIES FROM THE PAN LATER.

2. MELT THE BUTTER IN THE MICROWAVE OR IN A SMALL PAN OVER THE STOVE. TRANSFER THE MELTED BUTTER TO A MEDIUM SIZED BOWL.

3. ADD IN BOTH OF THE SUGARS AND USE A WHISK TO WHISK THE BUTTER AND SUGARS TOGETHER. KEEP WHISKING UNTIL THE MIXTURE RESEMBLES A PASTE THAT PULLS AWAY CLEANLY WHEN YOU MIX IT.

4. ADD THE EGGS AND VANILLA TO THE MIX AGAIN

5. POUR THE FLOUR AND SALT INTO THE BOWL AND MIX WITH THE WHISK UNTIL JUST COMBINED. (THIS SHOULD ONLY TAKE A MINUTE. DO NOT OVERMIX).

6. GENTLY FOLD THE CHOPPED CHOCOLATE UNTIL JUST COMBINED.

7. POUR THE BATTER INTO THE LINED BAKING PAN USING A SPATULA TO SCRAPE ALL THE BATTER OUT OF THE BOWL.

8. BAKE FOR 25-35 MINUTES. THE TOP OF THE BLONDIES SHOULD BE CRINKLY AND WHEN YOU INSERT A TOOTHPICK IN THE MIDDLE (IT SHOULD NOT COME OUT CLEAN) THEY ARE READY WHEN THERE ARE ONLY A FEW CRUMBS ON THE TOOTHPICK, BUT NOT WET BATTER.

52.

ALLYSIN KAY

Powerhouse wrestler Allysin Kay is slowly becoming a stalwart in women's wrestling in the United States. Debuting in 2008, the "AK47" is from Detroit, Michigan but has wrestled all over the world, including China, Japan, India, Canada, England, and Mexico. As a singles competitor, Kay has held multiple women's titles, including the defunct AIW Women's Championship where she's the longest reigning champion, TNA Women's Knockout Championship, a two-time Impact Knockouts Championship and SHINE Championship, NWA Women's Championship, AAW Women's Championship, GFW Women's Championship, and the CLASH Women's Championship.

Outside of singles competition, tag team wrestling has been equally important to Kay's career where she's wrestled in several teams over the course of it. Perhaps the most notable being The Hex with Marti Belle. The team first got its legs in SHINE Wrestling and SHIMMER, before quickly taking over the independent circuit in companies like NWA, ROH, Pro Wrestling: EVE, RevPro, Women's Wrestling Army (WWA), IMPACT, and more. The team has won various titles, including the NWA World Women's Tag Team Championships which they held for 287 days, after being defeated by Pretty Empowered at NWA Alwayz Ready in June of 2022.

Kay is also a big proponent of MMA. Initially starting to improve her wrestling ability, she eventually made her debut at Vertex Fight Night in Cadillac Michigan, where she won by a second round submission. Kay currently holds a 1-0 record. Her background helped earn her an opportunity to wrestle in Josh Barnett's Bloodsport II where she was the first female competitor to compete since its inception.

ALLYSIN KAY'S
EXTRA THICCCCCC CHEESECAKE

INGREDIENTS NEEDED:

- 2 C. CRUSHED CHOCOLATE COOKIES
- 1/4 C. BUTTER - MELTED
- 8 OZ. CREAM CHEESE, SOFTENED
- 1 C. SUGAR
- 1 1/2 TBSP. ALL-PURPOSE FLOUR
- 1/4 TSP. SALT
- 1 TSP. VANILLA
- 3 EGGS
- 2 TBSP. WHIPPING CREAM
- A SPLASH OF LEMON JUICE

INSTRUCTIONS

1. PREHEAT OVEN TO 450F
2. COMBINE COOKIE CRUMBS AND BUTTER; PRESS ONTO BOTTOM OF 9-INCH SPRINGFORM PAN
3. BEAT CREAM CHEESE LIKE IT OWES YOU MONEY (A BIG BOWL UNTIL CREAMY).
4. PRO TIP: LET CREAM CHEESE SOFTEN AT ROOM TEMPERATURE TO MAKE IT EASIER TO MIX. AS YOU START TO ADD THE NEXT INGREDIENTS, IT WILL START TO BECOME EASIER AS WELL. I HIGHLY RECOMMEND USING AN ELECTIC MIXER.
5. ADD SUGAR, FLOUR, SALT, AND VANILLA; MIX UNTIL ALL THE LUMPS ARE OUT.
6. ADD EGGS, ONE AT A TIME, BEATING WELL AFTER EACH ADDITION.
7. BLEND IN CREAM AND SPLASH OF LEMON JUICE.
8. REDUCE OVEN TEMPERATURE TO 200F; CONTINUE BAKING 25-40 MINUTES OR UNTIL SET
9. PRO TIP: THE TOP OF THE CHEESECAKE SHOULD LOOK FIRM BUT NOT TOO HARD OR BURNT.
10. LOOSEN CAKE FROM THE RIM OF THE PAN; COOL BEFORE REMOVING RIM OF PAN. REFRIGERATE.

ALTERNATIVE: YOU CAN ADD MANY TOPPINGS TO THIS CHEESECAKE AFTER COOLING AND BEFORE REFRIGERATING. STRAWBERRIES, CHOCOLATE DRIZZLE, CARAMEL, ETC.

PHOTO BY ALLYSIN KAY